BSCS Science T.R.A.C.S.

An Elementary School Science Program

Investigating Objects in the Sky

BSCS

KENDALL/HUNT PUBLISHING COMPANY
4050 Westmark Drive   Dubuque, Iowa 52002

BSCS Development Team

Nancy M. Landes, Project Director and Author, 1996–98
Gail C. Foster, Author
Colleen K. Steurer, Author
Vonna G. Pinney, Executive Assistant
Linda K. Ward, Senior Executive Assistant
Rodger W. Bybee, Principal Investigator, 1994–95
Harold Pratt, Project Director, 1994–96
Janet Chatlain Girard, Art Coordinator, 1994–96

BSCS Administrative Staff

Timothy H. Goldsmith, Chair, Board of Directors
Joseph D. McInerney, Director
Michael J. Dougherty, Assistant Director
Lynda B. Micikas, Assistant Director
Larry Satkowiak, Chief Financial Officer

Contributors/Consultants

Randall K. Backe, BSCS, Colorado Springs, Colorado
Judy L. Capra, Wheatridge, Colorado, free-lance writer
Michael J. Dougherty, BSCS, Colorado Springs, Colorado
B. Ellen Friedman, San Diego, California
Cathy Griswold, Lyons, Oregon
David A. Hanych, BSCS, Colorado Springs, Colorado
Jay Hackett, Greeley, Colorado
Debra A. Hannigan, Colorado Springs, Colorado, contributing author
Karen Hollweg, Washington, DC
Winston King, Bridgetown, Barbados

Paul Kuerbis, Colorado Springs, Colorado
Donald E. Maxwell, BSCS, Colorado Springs, Colorado
Marge Melle, Littleton, Colorado, free-lance writer
Lynda B. Micikas, BSCS, Colorado Springs, Colorado
Jean P. Milani, BSCS, Colorado Springs, Colorado
Renee Mitchell, Lakewood, Colorado, free-lance writer
Brenda S. McCreight, Colorado Springs, Colorado, contributing author
Mary McMillan, Boulder, Colorado
Carol D. Prekker, Broomfield, Colorado, contributing author
Patricia J. Smith, Tucson, Arizona, contributing author
Terry Spencer, Monterey, California, contributing author
Patti Thorn, Austin, Texas, contributing author
Bonnie Turnbull, Monument, Colorado, free-lance writer
Terri B. Weber, Colorado Springs, Colorado
Carol A. Nelson Woller, Boulder, Colorado, contributing author

Field-Test Teachers and Coordinators, Levels 1–3

Joanne Allen, Grade 3, Westport Elementary School, Westport, Maine
Helene Auger, Westport School District, Westport, Maine
Sheila Dallas, Grade 2, Bethany School, Cincinnati, Ohio

Library of Congress Catalog Card Number: 97-75499
ISBN 0-7872-2260-7

10 9 8 7 6 5 4 3 2 1

Pat Dobosenski, Grade 3, Pembroke Elementary School, Troy, Michigan

Nina Finkel, Grade 1, Whitter Elementary School, Chicago, Illinois

Mary Elizabeth France, Grade 2, Westport Elementary School, Westport, Maine

Carolyn Gardner, Grade 3, Calhan Elementary School, Calhan, Colorado

Shelly Gordon, Grade 2, Bingham Farms Elementary School, Birmingham, Michigan

Darlene Grunert, Birmingham Public Schools, Birmingham, Michigan

Terry Heinecke, Grade 1, Edgerton Elementary School, Kalispell, Montana

Katherine Hickey, Grade 1, Irving Primary School, Highland Park, New Jersey

Jan Himmelspach, Grade 1, Grayson Elementary School, Waterford, Michigan

Janet Smith-James, Grade 3, Bartle School, Highland Park, New Jersey

Elizabeth Lankes, Grade 3, Bethany School, Glendale, Ohio

Barbara O'Neal, Grade 1, Calhan Elementary School, Calhan, Colorado

Cheryl Pez, Grade 2, Bethany School, Cincinnati, Ohio

Rochelle Rubin, Waterford School District-IMC, Waterford, Michigan

Elizabeth A. Smith, Grade 3, Grayson Elementary School, Waterford, Michigan

Melanie W. Smith, Grade 2, Washington Elementary School, Raleigh, North Carolina

Catherine Snyder, Highland Park School District, Highland Park, New Jersey

Ingrid Snyder, Grade 1, Waterford Village School, Waterford, Michigan

Lee Ann Van Horn, Wake County Public School System, Raleigh, North Carolina

Kathy Wright, Calhan Elementary School, Calhan, Colorado

Reviewers, Levels 1–3

James P. Barufaldi, University of Texas, Austin, Texas

Larry W. Esposito, University of Colorado at Boulder, Boulder, Colorado

Brenda S. Evans, Department of Education, Raleigh, North Carolina

Randy Gray, National Weather Service, Pueblo, Colorado

Judith Johnson, University of Central Florida, Orlando, Florida

Eric Leonard, The Colorado College, Colorado Springs, Colorado

Brownie Linder, Northern Arizona University, Flagstaff, Arizona

Jerry Ludwig, Fox Lane High School, Bedford, New York

Mike Madsen, KKTV, Channel 11, Colorado Springs, Colorado

Kathleen Roth, Michigan State University, East Lansing, Michigan

Cherilynn A. Morrow, Space Science Institute, Boulder, Colorado

Barbara W. Saigo, Saiwood Biology Resources, Montgomery, Alabama

Gail Shroyer, Kansas State University, Manhattan, Kansas

Carol Snell, University of Central Florida, Orlando, Florida

Joseph Stepans, University of Wyoming, Laramie, Wyoming

Richard Storey, The Colorado College, Colorado Springs, Colorado

Joan Tephly, Marycrest University, Iowa City, Iowa

Jack Wheatley, North Carolina State University, Raleigh, North Carolina

CONTENTS

Investigating Objects in the Sky

Doing Science

What Is Science?

Read these questions. Write and draw pictures to show what you think.

1. What do people do when they do science?

2. What is a scientist like?

3. Can you be a scientist right now?

4. What would you be doing if you were doing science?

How Can You Do Science?

Wonder

Scientists wonder about the world around them. What do you wonder about?

Scientists ask questions about the world. What questions do you have about objects, animals, plants, or things that happen in the world around you?

Ask Questions

Scientists investigate to find answers to their questions. When they investigate, they often observe with their senses. Then, they describe and compare the objects, materials, and living things that they are investigating. Sometimes, they do something to the objects and find out what happens to them. Sometimes, they do a fair test and observe what happens. What questions would you like to investigate when you do science?

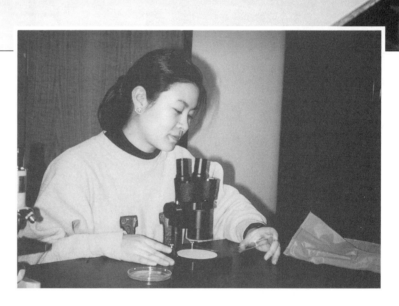

Use Tools

Scientists use tools, such as thermometers, magnifying glasses, microscopes, and rulers, to help them get information or **data** that they cannot get by using just their senses. What science tools have you used?

Scientists **record** the data from their investigations by writing, drawing, and making charts and graphs. These are the scientists' **records**. Scientists compare their records to the records of other scientists. How might you keep records of your investigations?

Keep Records

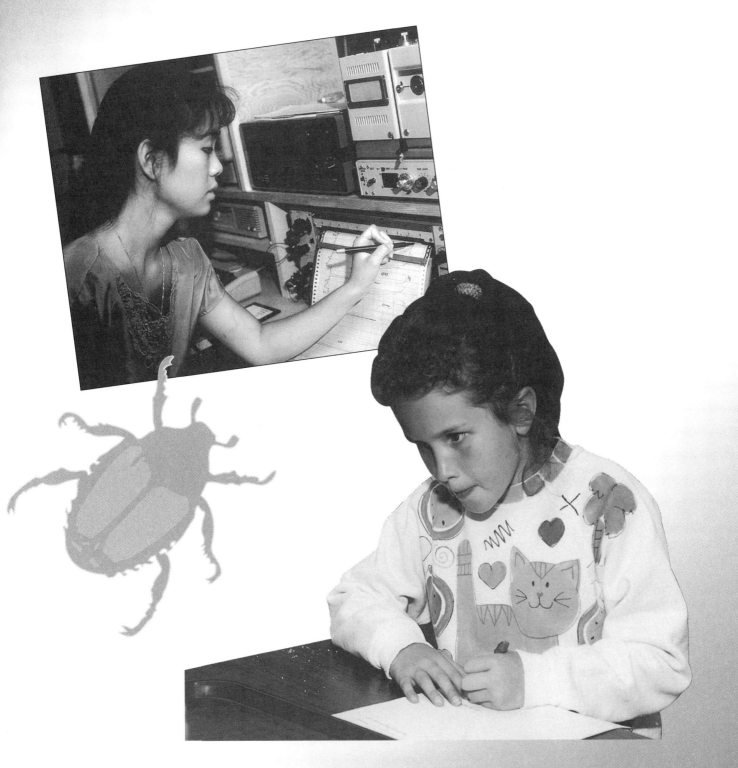

Share Your Ideas

One of the important jobs of a scientist is to explain how and why things happen in the world around us. They do investigations and use their records and data to help them explain things. They share and discuss their ideas with other scientists and with people who are not scientists, too. Sometimes they do their investigations again to find out if the same thing happens another time. Sometimes, other scientists do the same investigation. Then, the scientists compare what happened in all of the investigations. How can you share your ideas with others?

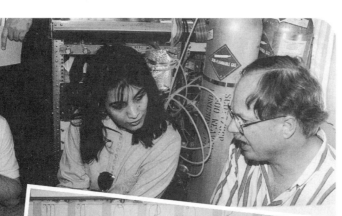

Wonder

Usually, when scientists do investigations, they think of new questions that they want to answer. Then, they do more investigations. Scientists never stop wondering about why things are the way they are.

Doing Science with C.Q. and I.O.

C.Q. and I.O. are characters in your student guide. Their job is to help you do science.

Working Together to Do Science

Scientists often work in teams so they can share ideas and tasks. In your student guide, C.Q. and I.O. usually work as a team. When you do science, you often will work in teams, too. Sometimes, you will work with your friends. Other times, you will work with teammates you don't know as well. You will stay in the same team through several lessons. Teammates have responsibilities.

All teammates are responsible for

- doing the task well, and
- helping their teammates understand the task and what the team did.

It is easier to do your team task well if you use some team skills while you work. Here are five team skills you will use every time you work in a team.

Team Skills

▶ Move into your teams quickly and quietly.

When your teacher tells you to meet with your team, find your teammates right away. Go directly to your team's meeting place without stopping to talk along the way.

▶ Stay with your teams.

This skill means that you pay attention to your teammates and work with them to do your task. You do not wander around the room and talk to other teams.

▶ Speak softly.

When you talk with your teammates, keep your voices down so only your teammates can hear you.

▶ Share and take turns.

The skill of sharing and taking turns is harder to use. You and your teammates must make sure that everyone on the team gets to do part of each investigation and to share their ideas. One way to make sure is to ask one another questions such as, "Have you had a chance to try this yet?" and "What do you think about it?"

▶ Do your job.

Manager

Tracker

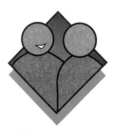

Messenger

To practice this skill, you need to know about three different jobs. You won't always have the same job. You might like one job more than the others, but each job is important for the team. You will have a chance to do all the jobs at some time.

Team Jobs

These job descriptions will help you remember what to do when it is your turn to do each job.

The **manager** gets the supplies that are listed in the Team Supplies section.

When the team finishes the team task, everyone helps clean up the work area. Then, the manager returns the supplies to the supply table.

The **tracker** keeps track of what the team is doing. The tracker makes sure that the team does every step and follows the directions in order.

The tracker might point to each step as the team works on it. If the team needs to stop, the tracker might write the number of the step where the team stopped. Everyone on the team needs to help read and follow the directions. The tracker is not the team's only reader.

The **messenger** may ask another team's messenger for help if the team gets stuck.

Or, the messenger may ask the teacher for help.

Only the messenger should go and ask for help, though. Everyone else should stay with the team.

Special Team Skills

Sometimes, your team will practice special skills that will help you work better together. Read the special skills and talk about them with your teacher. Describe what your team will say and do to practice each special skill.

▶ Ask for help and give help.

When might you ask for help? When might you offer help to a teammate?

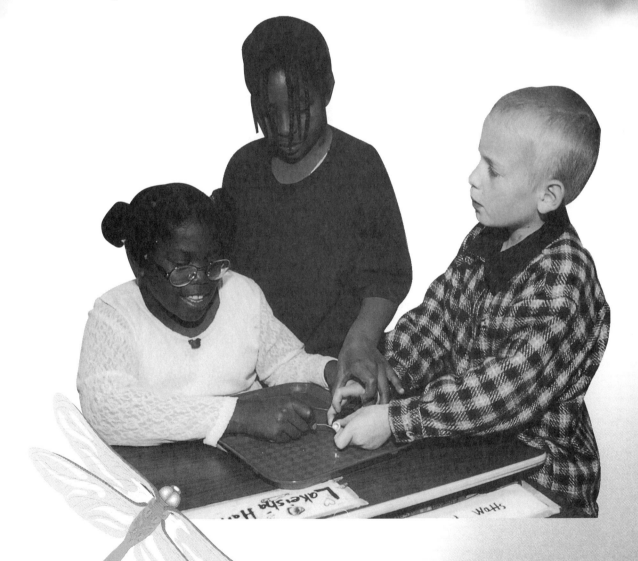

▶ Listen when others talk.

How can you show that you are really listening to a teammate? How can you make sure that every teammate has a chance to talk?

You will need to make a science journal to keep your records. A science journal is like a diary. It is a record you keep of what happens in an investigation. What you write in a journal also helps you remember what you did, what you observed, and when something happened. These pictures will help you remember when to record something, but you can use your journal other times, too.

Each time you check on an investigation, you can draw pictures, record measurements, and describe what you do or see in your journal. You can add special pages like calendar pages to your journal. The more information you record in your journal, the easier it will be to describe what happened in your investigation. You will use your records to help you explain why you think something happened, too.

In your journal, you can ask special questions you wonder about. Then, you can design your own investigations to find the answers to your special questions.

Invitation to Do Science

Are you curious about the world around you? If you are, then you are ready to do science. Remember to ask questions, investigate, and share your ideas. **You can find out a lot by doing science!**

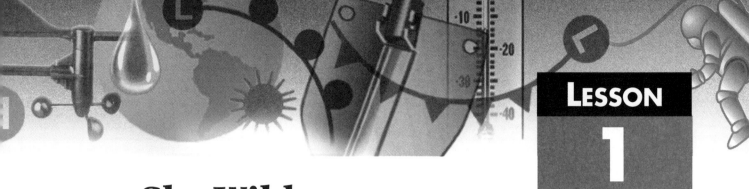

Sky Wilderness

If you looked at the sky on a clear, bright day, what would you see?

If you gazed at the sky on a clear, dark night, what would you see?

Draw one picture of what you would see in the daytime sky. Draw another picture of what you would see in the nighttime sky. Write words that describe the objects in the sky during the day and at night.

You can learn a lot about the objects in the sky just by watching them. As you observe the sky, you might be surprised by the objects that appear in the daytime and nighttime sky. You also might be surprised by all of the patterns you can find in the sky if you know how and where to look!

On Your Own

Drawing The Sky

Your Task
Read a story about a family that went on a camping trip. Draw what you think the sky looks like at each stopping place in the story.

Your Supplies

1 piece of drawing paper

1 ruler

markers or crayons

1 pencil

Directions for Drawing the Sky

1. Divide your paper into four sections and number them like this. Use your ruler to make straight lines.

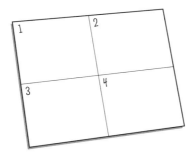

2. Read the story "The Camping Trip."

3. When you come to a (STOP) sign, stop and draw a picture of what you think the sky looks like to Chloe. Write the time of day or night on each drawing.

1 7:00 a.m.   2

3   4

You can write words that describe your pictures, too.

The Camping Trip

"It's summer vacation!" yelled Chloe and her little brother Sam as they ran barefoot through the house.

"Look out bears, here we come!" shouted Chloe.

"Look out buffalo, here we come!" echoed Sam as he followed Chloe.

They had been counting the days until their camping trip, and the day had finally come. Dad and Uncle Jordan had made all of the plans months ago.

"My duffel bag is packed!" Chloe called to her Dad. "I have all my clothes and a flashlight and...oh yeah...my toothbrush."

"Mine is packed, too," Sam said as he dragged his bag into the hallway. "I have my trucks, my alien spaceship, my superman cape, my Legos, some animal cookies, and my cowboy boots."

"Chloe, please help your brother get some clothes in his duffel bag while I finish putting the rest of the gear in the truck," Dad called from downstairs.

Dad looked at his watch as he and Uncle Jordan finished loading the tent and the camping gear. "It's 7:00 a.m. Right on time," he thought to himself. Then, he called toward the house, "Are you kids ready to roll?"

"Almost..." Sam mumbled, "but my space alien's foot is stuck in the zipper!"

"Here, I'll fix it," Chloe offered as she stuffed the alien's foot into the duffel bag and closed the zipper.

Uncle Jordan lifted Sam into the truck. "Fasten your safety belts, kids. We've got nine hours in the car before we get to Yellowstone Park." He smiled at Chloe and ruffled Sam's hair with one hand as he smoothed his mustache with his other hand.

Before Chloe stepped into the truck, she took a last look around. The sky looked like it usually did in the early morning. She didn't mind getting up early this time. They were going camping in Yellowstone National Park! STOP

Draw what you think the morning sky looked like to Chloe. What objects might she have seen in the sky at this time of day? In space #1 on your paper, draw those objects and show where they would be in the sky.

"Ready for take off?" Dad asked.

"READY!" yelled Chloe and Sam together as the truck pulled out of the driveway.

Chloe ignored her brother's endless stream of questions and looked out the window. They had been driving for several hours and had just entered the state of Wyoming. Chloe thought about the sky. It didn't look much different from the sky in Colorado, really. It was blue and big. Maybe it seemed like Wyoming's sky was bigger than Colorado's sky because there weren't any mountains in this place. The sky looked like it went on forever.

At noon, they stopped for lunch at a rest stop. Chloe looked around as she ate her sandwich. The Sun was in its usual place in the sky. It felt like summertime as they ate their lunch under the blue Wyoming sky. (STOP)

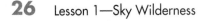

Draw what you think the sky looked like to Chloe at noon. What objects might she have seen in the sky at this time of day? In space #2 on your paper, draw those objects and show where they would be in the sky.

The truck whirred along at a steady pace for the rest of the afternoon with an occasional "leg stretcher." That's what Uncle Jordan called their breaks.

After a few more hours, they made it to Yellowstone Park. It was still light as the truck pulled into a wooded campsite.

As he stepped out of the truck, Uncle Jordan looked up at the sky and said, "Plenty of light left to get our camp set up and to cook dinner. Chloe and Sam, help me get the gear out of the car, please. I'm hungry!"

After they pitched their tents and Uncle Jordan got supper going, Chloe asked her Dad, "Is it okay if we walk toward the lake while dinner is cooking? I think it's just a little ways through the woods." Chloe's question hung in the air as Dad looked around the campsite and into the woods. Except for the sizzle of dinner on the camping stove, it was very quiet.

Chloe looked up at the sky as she waited for Dad's reply. It was evening, but still light enough to see. Dad looked at his watch and said, "Well, it's 7:30. I guess there's enough daylight left for you to explore a little."

Sam and Chloe pulled on sweatshirts and walked off into the woods. As they left the campsite, Uncle Jordan called, "Just don't fall into the lake. I don't want you to go swimming without me!" (STOP)

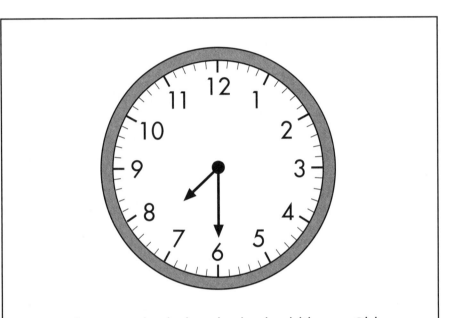

Draw what you think the sky looked like to Chloe at 7:30 in the evening. What objects might she have seen in the sky at this time of day? In space #3 on your paper, draw those objects and show where they would be in the sky.

"Walk quietly," Chloe ordered. "We don't want to scare anything."

Suddenly they both stopped, frozen in their tracks. "What's that?" Sam whispered to Chloe.

"I don't know," Chloe answered in a whisper. Her heart was pounding.

Crunch...Crunch...CRUNCH...CRUNCH... was all they heard. Footsteps...big footsteps...close footsteps. Somewhere just in front of them was something wild. Sam and Chloe slowly turned their heads back toward the campsite, then toward each other, then ahead of them to the place where they had heard the footsteps.

"What should we do, Chloe?" Sam's whisper shook with fear.

"Hey, you two softshoes, dinner's ready!" Uncle Jordan's voice called through the woods. At the sound of Uncle Jordan's voice, whatever made the footsteps took off running toward the lake. Sam and Chloe both sighed in relief and ran back toward the campsite.

"Something big is out there!" Sam yelled as he ran into the campsite. "Something with big teeth!"

"Sam, all we heard were footsteps. It could have been a chipmunk," Chloe said between heavy breaths. Her heart was pounding so hard she was sure both Dad and Uncle Jordan could hear it.

"Well, there's bound to be wildlife here. Hard to say what you heard." Uncle Jordan smiled quickly before putting a big spoonful of soup in his mouth. "Do you remember what we talked about? Always pay close attention. Be aware of where you are and what is around you. Turn on all your senses. We share this world with all kinds of living things. Don't get in the way or cause any harm to this place or to the animals that live here. If you do that, they won't harm you, okay?"

"Okay," Chloe and Sam both nodded at the same time.

"How about helping us get all the cooking gear and food loaded back into the truck. The park ranger came by and said there have been a few bear sightings. We need to keep the campsite clean to discourage furry visitors," Dad explained.

"Visitors? Bear visitors? Are there really bears here?" Chloe asked excitedly.

"Well, of course there are bears here. There also are buffalo, deer, chipmunks, moose, birds, foxes, wolves, and mosquitos," Uncle Jordan said as he slapped a mosquito that had landed on his neck.

"What did you expect—Disneyland? Let's get the place cleaned up and hit the sack. We have lots to do in the morning."

The sleeping bags were warm and the tent felt safe. An owl serenaded. Chloe and Sam drifted off to sleep in no time at all.

SCRATCH...Scratch...CRUNCH...CRUNCH...Crunch.

At first, Chloe didn't know if she was dreaming or awake. What was that noise? She felt her eyes to make sure they were open. They were open. She was definitely awake.

SCRATCH...SCRATCH...Crunch...Crunch....Then it was quiet.

"Uncle Jordan? Did you hear that noise?" Chloe whispered.

"I heard it," Uncle Jordan whispered. "Sounds like we've got visitors..."

"Can I unzip the tent and peek out?" Chloe asked with the familiar pounding in her chest.

"Go ahead...but quietly," Uncle Jordan whispered back. "It's 11:00, almost the middle of the night, and everyone else is sleeping."

Chloe slowly unzipped the tent and then stuck her head out. She looked up at the night sky. It was beautiful! She almost forgot why she had unzipped the tent. (STOP)

Draw what you think the sky looked like to Chloe at 11:00 at night. What objects might she have seen in the sky at this time of night? In space #4 on your paper, draw those objects and show where they would be in the sky.

Chloe looked and listened. It was quiet. Then, she heard breathing and crunch...crunch...scratch...scratch. Then, it was quiet again. She kept looking and listening.

Then, she saw them. Right beside the tent! The most beautiful doe and fawn she had ever seen. Their big, dark eyes looked at Chloe.

The doe went back to scratching the ground with her hoof, then nudged the fawn with her nose. Slowly, they walked away. The fawn looked back once, then both animals disappeared quietly into the woods.

Chloe watched as they walked away. She felt so happy. Her heart didn't pound and she wasn't afraid. Chloe turned and smiled toward Uncle Jordan, but he was snoring. She zipped the tent shut and fell back into her sleeping bag. "This is going to be the best summer vacation ever!" she thought as she drifted off to sleep.

Comparing Objects in the Sky

By now, you have read the story and drawn pictures of what you think the sky looks like in the morning, at noon, in the evening, and at night. Do you think your drawings look like the drawings of your classmates, or are they different? This activity will give you a chance to find out.

Team Task

Compare your drawings.
Share ideas about how the sky might have looked at each of the 🛑 places in the story. Tell why you think so.

Team Skills

Move into your teams quickly and quietly.
Stay with your team.
Speak softly.
Share and take turns.

Team Jobs

There are no jobs for this activity.

Team Supplies

drawings of the sky from
each teammate

markers or crayons

pencils

Take turns
reading. Each
teammate should
have a chance to
read.

Directions for Comparing Objects in the Sky

1. Read the story again.

2. When you come to a (STOP), share your drawings and compare your ideas about how the sky might look at that time.

3. You can add to or change the objects in your drawing if you think a teammate has a better idea.

Checking Understanding

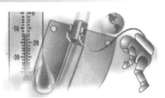

As a team, look at each teammate's drawings. Then write answers to these questions in your own journal.

1. List the objects that you can see in the daytime sky.

2. Did the objects in the sky look the same or different at (STOP) #1 and (STOP) #2?

   - How were they the same?
   - How were they different?

3. List the objects that you can see in the nighttime sky.

4. Did the sky objects look the same or different at (STOP) #3 and (STOP) #4?

   - How were they the same?
   - How were they different?

5. What can you find out about objects in the sky by observing them?

   - What would you like to find out about objects in the sky?
   - How might you find the answers to your questions?

It is all right to share ideas with your teammates before you record in your journal. Often, you get better ideas when you share.

6. Rate your teamwork.

Did you move into your team quickly
   and quietly?

Did you stay with your team?

Did you speak softly?

Did you share and take turns?

- Write one skill your team did well.
- Write one skill your team needs to improve.
- Write one way the team could do that skill better next time.

Moon Watching

Have you ever watched the Moon, your closest neighbor in space? Can you see the Moon every night? What does it look like? Try "Moon Watching," especially when the night sky is clear. You don't need any special equipment to be a Moon Watcher . . . just use your senses!

On Your Own

What Do You Know About the Moon?

Your Task
Show what you know about the Moon by writing and drawing in your journal.

Your Supplies

your science journal

markers or crayons

pencil

Directions for What Do You Know About the Moon?

In your journal, write or draw your answers to these questions.

1. Have you ever seen the Moon in the daytime? If so, draw what it looked like.

2. Have you ever seen the Moon at night? If so, draw what it looked like.

3. What is the shape of the Moon? Does it have more than one shape?

4. Why do you think the Moon looks different at different times?

5. Is the Moon always in the same place or do you see it in different places at different times? Tell where you have seen the Moon in the sky.

6. Write or draw anything else you know about the Moon.

Moon Watching

In this lesson, you will try to find the Moon during the day with your teammates. You will try to find the Moon on your own (with an adult!) in the evening. Each time you "Moon watch," make drawings and write notes in your journal about what you see. You can write or draw on a Moon Calendar, on a note page, or on drawing paper. Watching the Moon for many days and nights will help you find out more about it.

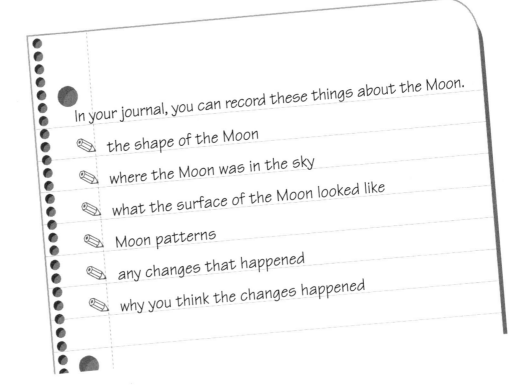

In your journal, you can record these things about the Moon.

- the shape of the Moon
- where the Moon was in the sky
- what the surface of the Moon looked like
- Moon patterns
- any changes that happened
- why you think the changes happened

What other things about the Moon would you like to record in your journal? You can record anything you observed about the Moon or write any questions you would like to answer.

Becoming Moon Watchers

As you Moon watch, you will be working like real scientists who study the sky. Scientists who study objects in the sky are called **astronomers**.

Sometimes, clouds might block your view of the Moon. Sometimes, you won't be able to watch the Moon because it rises after you are in bed. All good astronomers know that they can't change the weather or the way things happen in the sky. They just have to wait and watch whenever they can!

Team Task
Try to find the Moon in the daytime sky every day for one month. Record on a Day Moon Calendar what the Moon looked like. Write other notes in your journal.

Team Skill

Share and take turns.

Team Jobs

There are no jobs for this activity.

Team Supplies

each teammate's science
   journal

3 copies of the Day Moon
   Calendar

3 pencils

Be sure to leave enough room to draw the Moon in the square, too.

Directions for Becoming Moon Watchers

1. In your journal, leave space for writing notes about the Moon every day.

On your Day Moon Calendar, write the date and time in the first square.

2. Take your calendar page and journal outside. If you see the Moon, draw its shape exactly as you see it. If you do not see the Moon, say so on your calendar page.

3. If you see the Moon, use hand measures as shown on pages 46 and 47 to find the Moon's sky position. Record the Moon's sky position in your journal.

4. Record the Moon's sky direction in your journal.

   - Is the Moon in the northern sky, the eastern sky, the southern sky, the western sky, or directly overhead?

   - Decide on a building or another landmark outside. Describe the position of the Moon from that object. For example, is it above, to the left of, or to the right of the object?

If you are not sure about the sky direction, ask your teacher for help.

5. Record notes about the weather or anything else you want to remember about the Moon on this day.

6. Repeat Steps 1–5 for each day on your Day Moon Calendar.

   - Choose a teammate to observe the Moon on Saturday and Sunday.

   - Share the information and record it in your journal.

Use Your Hands and Find The Moon's Sky Position

Put your arms out straight with your palms facing you. Put the fingers of each hand together tightly and point your thumbs straight up. Put one hand above the other one so that your hands are touching.

Keep your hands on top of each other. Move your hands until the little finger of the bottom hand looks like it is lying on the ground. Line your hands up with the Moon. In this picture, the Moon is two hands high.

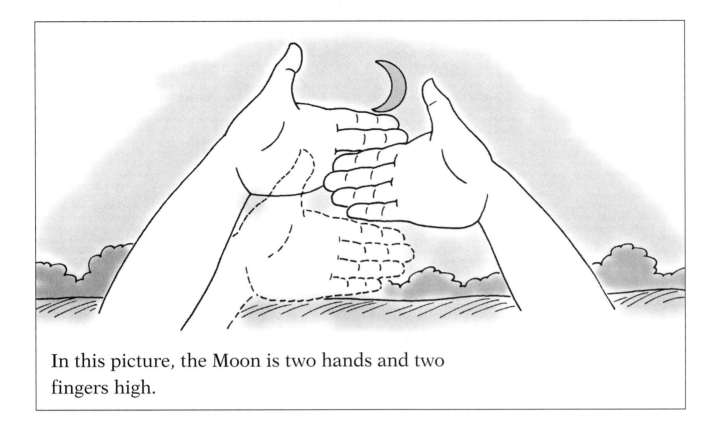

In this picture, the Moon is two hands and two fingers high.

On Your Own

Watching the Moon at Night

Your Task

Try to observe the Moon every night for at least one month.

Record what you observe on a Night Moon Calendar.

Keep notes in your journal, too.

Your Supplies

your science journal   pencil

1 Night Moon Calendar

Directions for Watching the Moon at Night

Look for the Moon each night. Take an adult with you! Before you Moon watch, write the date and time on your Night Moon Calendar. If you see the Moon, draw a picture on your calendar of what the Moon looks like. Try to show the exact shape of the Moon. If you do not see the Moon, record that you could not find the Moon on that night.

Use your hands to measure the Moon's sky position. Record the Moon's sky position and sky direction in your journal. Make notes about the weather. Be ready to share your drawings and notes with the class.

Checking Understanding

Every day and night that you Moon watch, your teacher will choose a team to tell about the Moon and fill in the class chart. When it is your team's turn, draw the shape of the Moon on the class chart and share the notes from your journal. Compare your team's drawings and notes with those from other teams.

After you have observed the Moon for one week, predict what you think the Moon will look like the next day or the next night. Draw your prediction and find out by observing.

After you have observed the Moon for at least one month, write about these questions in your journal.

1. How many different Moon shapes did you see?

2. In what order did the shapes of the Moon appear?

3. Is there a pattern in the shapes that you observed? If so, describe the pattern.

4. Did the Moon always have the same sky position and direction?

5. Is there a pattern in the Moon's sky position? If so, what is the pattern?

6. What is the shape of the Moon? Why do you think it looks different from one day to the next?

Do You Have a Moon Imagination?

The light and dark patches on the Moon look like various creatures to different people in different parts of the world. Look closely the next time you see the big, round, full Moon. Turn on your Moon imagination!

Can you see the eyes, nose, and mouth of the man (or woman) in the Moon? Many people in the United States can.

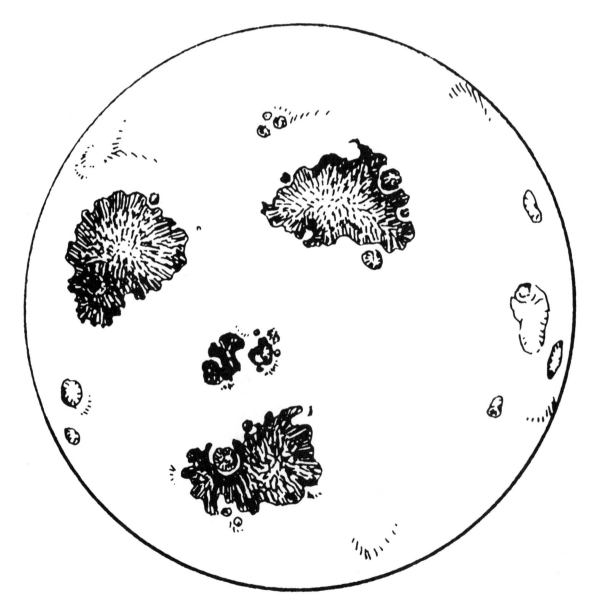

Can you see a long-eared rabbit, facing sideways? Many people in Japan can.

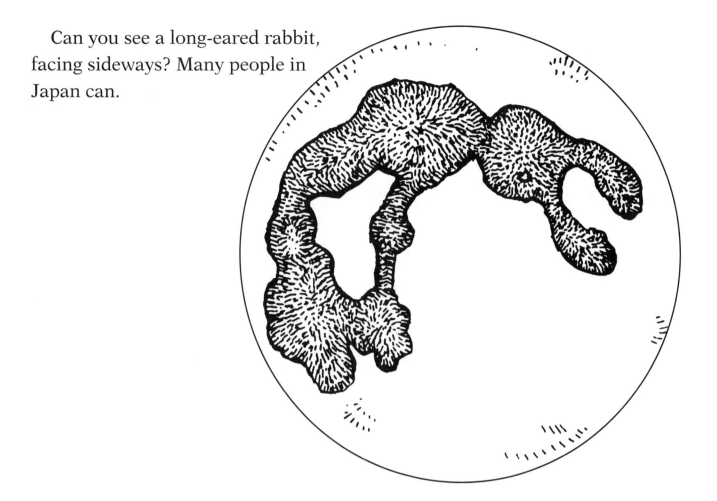

Can you see a boy and a girl carrying a bucket between them? The people in Scandinavia do. To Scandinavian children, the Moon pictures look like "Jack and Jill" from the nursery rhyme.

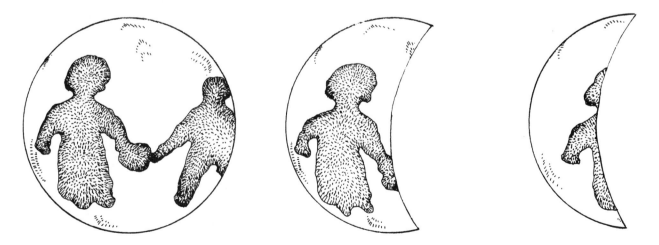

What can you see on the surface of the Moon? Use your Moon imagination!

Moon Facts

- The Moon is the same age as Earth—more than 4 billion years old.

- There are craters on the Moon's surface. Some craters are the size of small states, such as Delaware or Rhode Island. The craters were made when meteors or asteroids hit the surface of the Moon.

- There are sharp, jagged mountain ranges on the Moon. The Moon's tallest mountain is higher than Mt. Everest, the tallest mountain on Earth.

- The dark patches you see when you look at the Moon are called **maria**. Maria is the Latin word for "seas" or oceans. Maria are not real seas because there is no water anywhere on the Moon.

- There is no air, no wind, and no noise on the Moon.

- The temperature on the Moon may be as hot as a baking oven or as cold as ice.

- The Moon does not have its own light. "Moonlight" is really sunlight reflecting off the Moon.

- On July 20, 1969, the first United States astronauts walked on the Moon. Astronauts who landed on the Moon in later missions rode in an electric dune buggy called a Lunar Rover.

The Wind and the Moon

by George MacDonald

As you read this poem, try to figure out how the Moon must look. Which verses describe the shapes of the Moon that you have seen?

Said the Wind to the Moon, "I will blow you out;
You stare
In the air
Like a ghost in a chair,
Always looking what I am about;
I hate to be watched; I will blow you out."

The Wind blew hard, and out went the Moon.
So, deep
On a heap
Of clouds to sleep,
Down lay the Wind, and slumbered soon—
Muttering low, "I've done for that Moon."

He turned in his bed; she was there again!
On high
In the sky,
With her one ghost eye.
The Moon shone white and alive and plain
Said the Wind—"I'll blow you out again."

The Wind blew hard, and the Moon grew dim
"With my sledge
And my wedge
I have knocked off her edge!
If only I blow right fierce and grim,
The creature will soon be dimmer than dim."

He blew and he blew,
and she thinned to a thread.
"One puff
More's enough
To blow her to snuff!
One good puff more where the last was bred,
And glimmer, glimmer, glum will go that thread!"

He blew a great blast and the thread was gone.
In the air
Nowhere

Was a Moonbeam bare;
Far-off and harmless the shy stars shone;
Sure and certain the Moon was gone!

The Wind he took to his revels once more;
On down,
In a town,
Like a merry-mad clown,
He clapped and halloed with whistle and
roar—
"What's that?" The glimmering thread once
more!

He flew in a rage—he danced and he blew;
But in vain
Was the pain
Of his bursting brain;
For still the broader the Moon-scrap grew
The broader he swelled his big cheeks and blew.

Slowly she grew—till she filled the night,
And shone
On her throne
In the sky alone,
A matchless, wonderful, silvery light,
Radiant and lovely, the Queen of the night.

Said the Wind, "What a marvel of power am I!
With my breath
Good faith,
I blew her to death—
First blew her away right out of the sky—
Then blew her in; what a strength am I!"

But the Moon she knew nothing about the affair;
For high
In the sky,
With her one white eye,
Motionless, miles above the air,
She had never heard the great
Wind blare.

Changes in Shadows

My Shadow

by Robert Louis Stevenson

I have a little shadow that goes
in and out with me,
And what can be the use of him
is more than I can see.
He is very, very like me from the heels
up to the head;
And I see him jump before me, when I
jump into my bed.
The funniest thing about him is
the way he likes to grow—
Not at all like proper children, which
is always very slow;
For he sometimes shoots up taller
like an India-rubber ball,
And he sometimes gets so little that there's
none of him at all.
One morning, very early, before the
sun was up,
I rose and found the shining dew
on every buttercup;
But my lazy little shadow, like an
arrant sleepy head,
Had stayed at home behind me
and was fast asleep in bed.

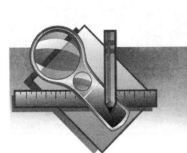

Shadow Fun

Sometimes, you have a shadow. Sometimes, animals have shadows. Sometimes, trees, bicycles, and cars have shadows. Clouds and airplanes can have shadows, too. In fact, almost everything can have a shadow.

Why do people, animals, and objects have shadows? Are shadows always the same size? Why do you think so?

How well do you think you know your own shadow?
Go outside and find out!

Your Task
Observe and describe your shadow. Make changes in your shadow.

Your Supplies

your science journal

a pencil, crayon, or marker

one sunny day

Directions for Shadow Fun

1. Investigate your shadow by doing these things.

   • Describe your shadow. (Does it look like you?
     What is the same? What is different?)

- Make your shadow disappear.

- Put your shadow in front of you, behind you, beside you.

- Put your shadow under you.

- Make your shadow bigger, smaller, taller, or shorter.

- Make your shadow taller than you are.

- Make your shadow shorter than you are.

- Stand still and describe what your shadow does.

- Move around and describe what your shadow does.

- Close your eyes and turn around. Keep your eyes closed and point to where you think your shadow is. Open your eyes. Are you right?

2. Get together with some classmates.

Make your shadows into something special.

Sharing
IDEAS

Talk about the answers to these questions with your classmates.

1. What did your shadow look like?

2. What caused your shadow to change? Why do you think so?

3. How did you make your shadow change positions? How did you put it in front of you? How did you put it behind you?

4. What do you think makes shadows?

5. Do you think you can make shadows inside or at night? Why do you think so?

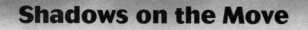

Shadows on the Move

You have investigated ways to change your shadow as you moved around. Do you think your shadow can change if you don't move at all? Make a prediction in your science journal. Then, try it and find out what happens.

Team Skill

Do your job.

Team Jobs

Manager

Tracker

Messenger

Team Supplies

2 pieces of different colored chalk	each teammate's science journal
1 Shadows on the Move Record Page	1 pencil
1 tape measure	

Bring all of your supplies, too.

Directions for Shadows on the Move

1. Go outside with your team.

2. Record the time of day at Time 1 on your record page.

3. Manager: Do these things.

- Stand with your shadow in front of you.
- Stand with your feet together.
- Stand straight and tall.
- Stand very still!

4. Messenger: Trace around the manager's feet using one color of chalk.

5. Tracker: Trace all the way around the manager's shadow using the same color of chalk.

6. Find out where the Sun is in the sky. Record the Sun's sky position on your record page.

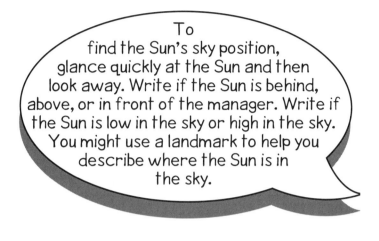

To find the Sun's sky position, glance quickly at the Sun and then look away. Write if the Sun is behind, above, or in front of the manager. Write if the Sun is low in the sky or high in the sky. You might use a landmark to help you describe where the Sun is in the sky.

CAUTION

NEVER look directly at the Sun with your eyes, even through sunglasses. NEVER look at the Sun through binoculars or through a telescope. The Sun is so bright that it can hurt your eyes or even blind you. Be very careful when you find the Sun's sky position.

7. Go inside and wait at least one hour.

8. In your science journal, predict if the manager's shadow will change when you go back outside. If you think it will change, write or draw what you think the shadow will look like.

Later.....

9. When the team goes outside again, record the time of day at Time 2. Record the Sun's position in the sky.

Is the Sun in the same place as it was before? Is it behind, above, or in front of the manager? How high is it in the sky?

10. The manager should stand in the <u>same</u> footprints, facing exactly the same way as before.

Why do you think the manager should stand in exactly the same place?

11. Messenger and Tracker: Use a different color of chalk and trace the manager's shadow.

12. Look at the outlines of the two shadows. Talk about these questions with your teammates.

 • Did the shadow change from Time 1 to Time 2?

 • How do you know?

 • How much did it change?

 • What tool can you use to find out?

13. Finish your record page.

Checking Understanding

 Talk about the Sun and shadows with your teammates. Write your answers in your own journal.

1. What changes did you observe in the manager's shadow?

2. What changes did you observe in the Sun's sky position?

3. Why do you think the manager's shadow changed, even when the manager stood in the same footprints?

4. If you went outside to trace the manager's shadow again, how do you think the manager's shadow would have changed?

5. If you went outside to trace the manager's shadow again, how do you think the Sun's position would have changed?

6. Share your ideas with other teams.

   Does every team have the same ideas?

   How might you test your ideas?

What do you know about the Sun that shines in the sky?

What is the shape of the Sun? Does it ever look a different shape like the Moon does?

Is the Sun like the Moon? Is it different from the Moon?

What do you think happens to the Sun at night?

What do you think would happen to someone's shadow from morning until night?

- Would the shadow stay the same?
- Would the shadow get shorter?
- Would the shadow get longer?
- Would the shadow change directions?
- Would the shadow be the same every morning at 10 o'clock?

Draw a picture to show what you think. Then, do an investigation to find out!

Is the Sun ever directly overhead at noon? Is the Sun in the same position at noon every day or does it change?

What else would you like to know about the Sun and shadows? Write your questions in your journal. Decide how you could find out.

Ideas to Think
ABOUT

People living in Egypt long ago worried when they could not see the Sun at night. They believed that when daytime ended, the Sun had to travel through an underground cave and fight off demons before it could come back the next morning.

People living in China long ago believed that the Sun disappeared at night because a giant dragon chased the Sun from the sky.

What do you think about these explanations? Can you find other "Sun Stories" from other cultures? Why do you think people do not believe these stories about the Sun any more?

Sun Facts

☀ The Sun has been shining for 4.5 billion years.

☀ Our Sun is a star. Stars are huge balls of churning, glowing gases. We can see many stars at night, but the Sun is the only star we can see during the daytime. Why do you think we cannot see other stars during the daytime?

☀ The Sun is very HOT! At its center, it might be 27 million degrees Fahrenheit!

☀ The Sun does not burn in the same way that a fire does. It is much hotter than a fire. Deep inside the Sun, one kind of gas is changing into a different kind of gas. This is how the Sun makes the light and heat we receive on Earth.

☀ The Sun is huge compared to Earth or the Moon, but it is called a *yellow dwarf star*. Compared to other stars, the Sun is small and yellow. It looks larger to us than other stars because it is so close to Earth.

☀ To study the Sun safely, astronomers use special solar telescopes. The telescopes have filters and mirrors that focus an image of the Sun onto a viewing table. Solar telescopes are on high mountaintops because astronomers need cloudless skies to observe the Sun.

☀ Sometimes the Sun has dark freckles, called sunspots, on its surface. Scientists don't understand sunspots completely. They don't know exactly how or why they form. Sunspots usually last for about a week, but some may last many months before they disappear.

☀ The Sun gives us light and heat. Without light and heat from the Sun, there would be no food, weather, or energy. Without the Sun, there would be no life on Earth. Earth would be nothing but a hunk of rock.

☀ In 1990, NASA launched a spacecraft named Ulysses. Ulysses is orbiting the Sun! By the end of its journey, Ulysses will give scientists a lot of new information about the Sun.

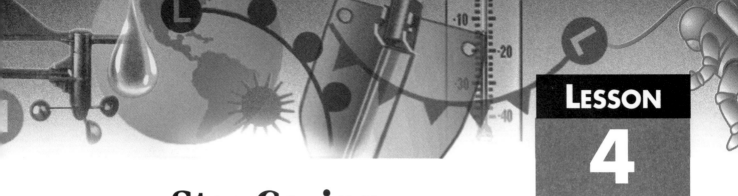

Star Gazing

After the sky becomes dark, points of light twinkle in the sky. The sky is full of stars!

Star Pictures

People who lived long ago looked at the stars a lot. As they looked, they realized that not all stars looked the same. Some stars appeared brighter to them than others, and some stars appeared to be different colors. They even saw groups of stars in the sky that seemed to form pictures. They imagined the star pictures to be things that were familiar to them, such as tools, animals, gods, imaginary creatures, and story heroes.

The star pictures were very important to people of long ago. They named the star pictures and told stories about how they came to be in the sky. We call those star pictures **constellations**. Many constellations still have the names that people gave them long ago.

Have you ever tried to find a constellation? When you look for constellations, you have to use your imagination, just as people did long ago.

What picture do you think people saw in this group of stars? What picture do you see?

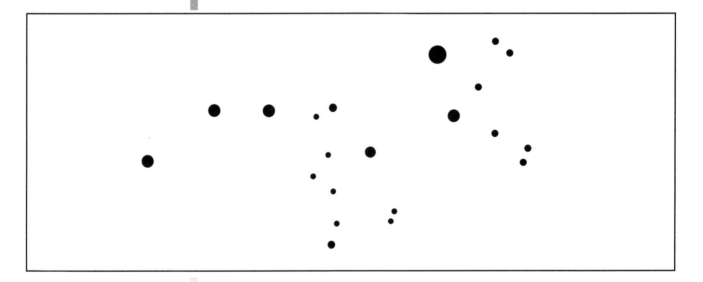

People in different parts of the world have seen different pictures in this group of stars. They tell different stories about this constellation.

In a story told by the Greeks, Hera, the queen of the gods, was very jealous of a beautiful young woman named Callisto. She was so jealous that she wanted to kill Callisto. But Zeus, king of the gods, was very fond of Callisto and wanted to protect her from Hera. To protect her, he changed Callisto into a bear. Then, to keep hunters from shooting her in the forest, he held her by her tail and twirled her into the sky. Can you use your imagination to see what the Greeks saw?

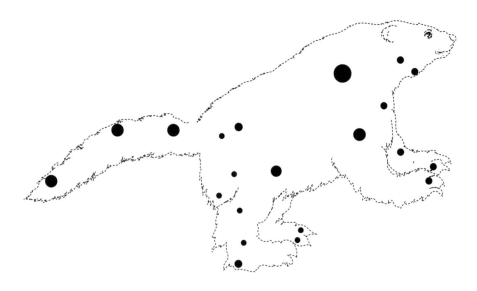

In another story told by the Zuni Indians, the Great Bear protected them from snow and ice. During spring, summer, and fall, the fierce bear kept the ice gods away from their land. But during the winter, when the Great Bear hibernated, the frozen breath of the ice gods attacked the Zuni's land. They were not safe from the ice gods until the springtime thunder filled the sky. This, the Indians believed, was the sign that the Great Bear was waking from its sleep and beginning to growl. His fierce growling drove the ice gods back to the north where they belonged, and the Zuni's land once again was under the protection of the Great Bear.

Some people still call this group of stars **Ursa Major**, the Great Bear. The star pattern has another, more familiar, name that you will read about in Lesson 5.

Making Constellations in a Can

Now you and your teammates can make a constellation and draw what you see in the stars. When you are finished, you can find out about lots of other constellations by looking at other teams' constellations and star drawings.

Team Task
Make a "constellation in a can" and put on a star show!

Team Skill

Ask for help and give help.

Team Jobs

Manager   Tracker   Messenger

Team Supplies

1 empty coffee can with a plastic lid	2 pieces of black construction paper
1 cardboard circle	1 flashlight
2 copies of one constellation pattern	markers
1 pushpin	each teammate's science journal
tape	3 pencils

Directions for Making Constellations in a Can

1. **Manager:** Place one of the star patterns on top of the cardboard circle. Hold the pattern in place so it does not move.

2. **Tracker:** Using a sharp pencil, mark the stars of the constellation through the paper onto the cardboard.

3. Tape the cardboard over one end of the can. Make sure the pencil pattern is on the **outside** of the can.

4. Tracker: Use the pushpin and *carefully* punch holes through all the pencil marks on the cardboard. Twist the pushpin while it is in the cardboard to make the holes as round and smooth as possible.

5. Use a pencil point to make the holes larger for the brightest stars.

6. Fasten two pieces of black construction paper together with tape. Roll the construction paper into a tube and place it inside the can. The paper should line the inside of the can.

7. Place the plastic lid on the other end of the can.

8. Put the flashlight into the can through the hole in the plastic lid.

If your team finishes before the others, begin the next activity, Star Pictures.

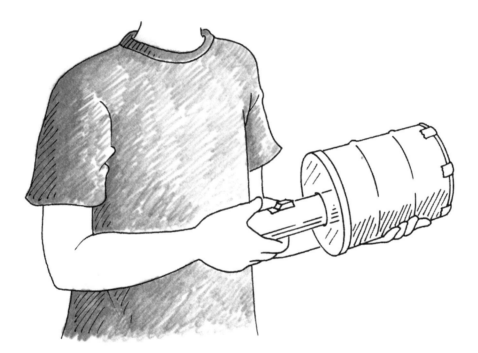

9. When all teams are ready, put on a star show!

- When your teacher tells you, point the can at a wall or at the ceiling.

- Turn on the flashlight.

- Take turns showing your constellation.

Star Pictures

Your team should have an extra copy of the star pattern that you can share. Look carefully at the star pattern and copy it into your science journal.

What does the pattern look like to you? On your own, draw a picture using the star pattern. You do not have to use all of the stars in your design. When you finish your drawing, give your constellation a name. Compare your drawings and names for the constellation with your teammates.

Write a story about the picture you drew and tell how your constellation came to be in the sky.

Tape all teammates' star pictures and stories onto a piece of construction paper and make a poster.

Be ready to tell your classmates about your constellation.

Star Finders

Is your constellation really in the sky? How can you find out?

What we need is a road map of the whole sky!

You've got to be kidding, C.Q.! Where would we get a map of the sky?

It might seem strange, but there **are** maps of the sky. Looking at a star map of the night sky can help you find different constellations. If you know where to look, you can find almost any constellation on a star map. The star map can help you find the same constellation in the night sky.

Team Task

Find your team's star picture on two different star maps.

Fill in your team's record page.

Team Skill

Ask for help and give help.

Team Jobs

Manager

Tracker

Messenger

Team Supplies

a copy of your team's star pattern	Star Finder Record Page
Star Map 1	pencil
Star Map 2	

Directions for Star Finders

1. Look closely at your team's star pattern.

2. Look closely at Star Map 1.

3. Match your team's star pattern to a constellation shown on Star Map 1.

4. On your record page, write the name of the star pattern from Star Map 1.

5. Find the names of two star patterns that are near your star pattern on Star Map 1. Write those names on your record page.

6. Get Star Map 2. Match your team's star pattern to a constellation shown on Star Map 2.

7. On your record page, write the name of the star pattern that is shown on Star Map 2.

8. Find the names of two star patterns that are near your star pattern on Star Map 2. Write those names on your record page.

Sharing
IDEAS

1. How did you find your star pattern on each of the star maps?

2. How many of the stars in your star pattern were shown on each of the star maps?

3. Was the name of your star pattern the same on Star Map 1 and Star Map 2? If not, why do you think the names were different?

4. Was your star pattern next to the same or different star patterns on Star Map 1 and Star Map 2? Why do you think so?

5. Do you think your star pattern always has the same sky place? Tell why you think so.

6. What happens to the stars during the day? (Hint: Think about what happens when you turn on the classroom lights and show your constellations in a can. Can you see your star pattern?)

7. How are the stars in your constellation in a can different from real stars?

Star Facts

★ The stars we see in the night sky are like the Sun. Some are larger than the Sun and some are smaller. They look tiny because they are so far away compared to the Sun.

★ Stars are very far away from Earth. The nearest star (other than our Sun) is named Proxima Centauri. It is 25 trillion (25,000,000,000,000) miles away. If we sent one of our spaceships to this star system, it would take hundreds and hundreds of years for it to get there.

★ Like the Sun, ALL stars are hot balls of glowing gases. Blue-white stars are the hottest stars. Yellow-orange ones, like the Sun, are not quite so hot. Red stars are the least hot of all.

★ The brightest star in the nighttime sky is Sirius. It is sometimes called the Dog Star because it is in the constellation Canus Major, the Big Dog.

★ From Earth, all the stars in a constellation appear to be close together. But, stars within constellations are not always what they seem—they might be very far apart!

★ Today, astronomers officially recognize 88 constellations. When combined, these constellations cover the whole sky. How many constellations do you know?

Star Guides

Now that you know about constellations and where you can find them on a star map, it's time for some **real** stargazing in the nighttime sky.

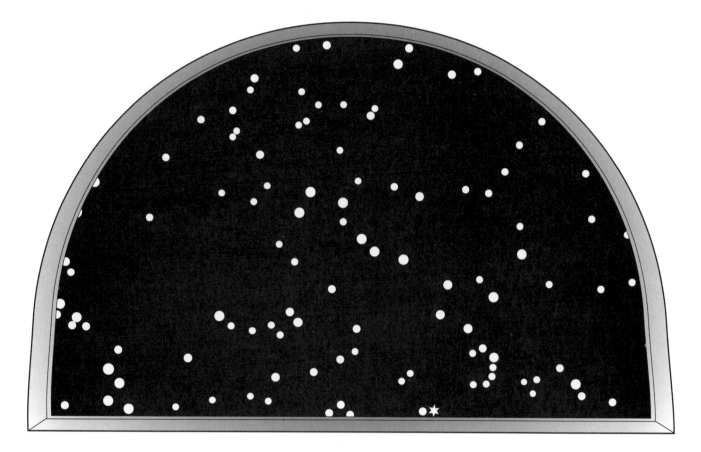

When you first look at the night sky, it can be difficult to find constellations. There are so many stars in the sky! On a clear evening, you might see thousands of stars if the Moon isn't too bright. Also, the constellations in the real sky look a little different from those on a star map.

So, to help you find your way around the real night sky, you will need a guide—a star guide. This guide is made of seven stars. The stars are fairly bright and easy to spot. You probably know the star guide's shape. It looks like this.

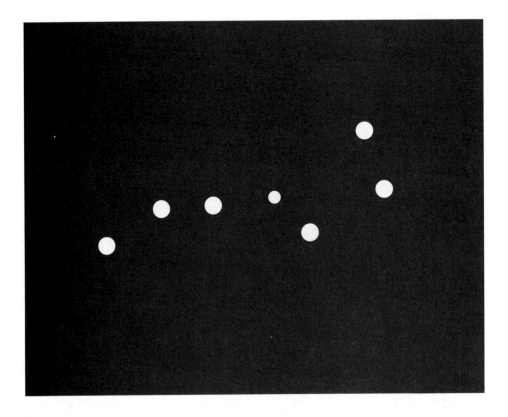

People have used this constellation as a guide for thousands of years. This star guide is part of a larger constellation that you observed in Lesson 4. It is called Ursa Major, the Great Bear. Look back in Lesson 4. Can you find the seven stars in the picture of Ursa Major on page 75?

People in different parts of the world see different pictures when they look at this star guide. The Iroquois Indians see a bear hunted by three Indian braves. This is the story they tell about this constellation.

Once upon a time in a strange land, a group of Indian braves was hunting a bear in the forest. The braves ran into three angry giants who killed all but three of them. Suddenly, those three Indians went into the sky along with the bear. The Indian braves continue to hunt the bear in the sky today.

The Iroquois see a bear in the four stars that form a rectangle. The three stars next to the rectangle are the three Indian braves. They believe that the brave closest to the bear carries a bow with which to shoot the bear. The next Indian carries a pot in which to boil the bear. The third Indian brave carries wood to light the fire.

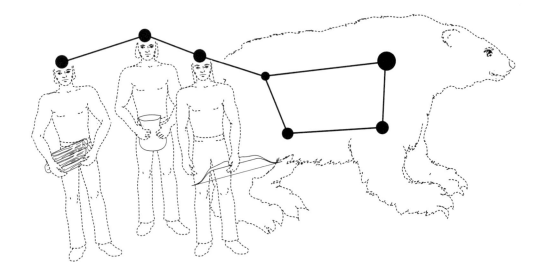

Long ago, the people living in Rome saw seven oxen in the same constellation. The Germans and Babylonians saw a big wagon.

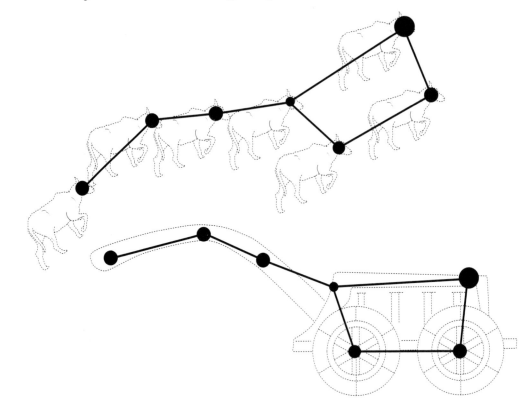

Many people today think that the seven stars of the star guide form the outline of a dipper. They call it the Big Dipper. What do you know about the Big Dipper?

The Big Dipper is an important guide for finding your way around the night sky. It can be used as a compass because it always shows which direction is north.

Polaris, the North Star

Little Dipper (Ursa Minor)

Big Dipper (Ursa Major)

the pointer stars

If you draw a line from the two stars in the front of the bowl of the Big Dipper, the stars point north, toward a very important star. This star is Polaris, the North Star.

The North Star has no stars around it, so it's usually easy to find. Polaris is over Earth's North Pole. When you face the North Star, you are facing true north. Long ago, people traveling on the sea and over land learned how to tell directions by using this important star. By knowing where the North Star was, they knew which direction was north. Then, they could find other directions, too.

Polaris also helped travelers figure out how far north of the Equator they were. How high Polaris is above the horizon is equal to the **latitude**. Look at a map or a globe and find the latitude lines. Do you think the North Star would appear higher or lower in the sky as you moved closer to the Equator?

Think of it, C.Q.! Without the Big Dipper and the North Star, people of long ago would not have known which direction they were going!

Do you suppose they got lost when it was cloudy at night?

Get with your team and find the Big Dipper, its pointer stars, and the North Star on your star maps. Draw the stars in your sky journal. Then, find a constellation shaped like a "W." That constellation is called Cassiopeia. When you find it, draw Cassiopeia in your journal, too. Try to draw the constellations in their correct sky places.

Cassiopeia...Hmmm. I'll bet there's a good story behind that name.

Making a Dipper and Queen Finder

Since the Big Dipper is your star guide, it's important to find it easily. It's also fun to find a neighboring constellation, Queen Cassiopeia. You can make a Dipper and Queen Finder to help you. When you are finished, you can use this special tool to find the Big Dipper and the Queen Cassiopeia in the night sky.

Team Task

Make a Dipper and Queen Finder for each teammate. Practice using them in the classroom.

Team Skill

Ask for help and give help.

Team Jobs

Manager

Tracker

Messenger

Team Supplies

3 patterns for the Dipper and Queen Finder	glue
3 pieces of thin cardboard	3 pairs of scissors
3 paper fasteners	pencils
1 pushpin	

Directions for Making a Dipper and Queen Finder

1. Cut out the circle and rectangle from the pattern.

2. Glue each piece of the pattern to a piece of cardboard. Cut out the cardboard patterns.

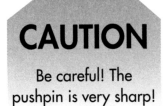
3. Use the pushpin to poke holes in the center of each pattern.

4. Place the circle on top of the rectangle. Fasten the pieces together by putting a paper fastener through the North Star (Polaris).

5. Watch as your teacher shows you how to use the Dipper and Queen Finder.

6. Practice using your Dipper and Queen Finder.

- Ask for help if you need help.

- Help your teammates if they need help.

The Legend of Queen Cassiopeia

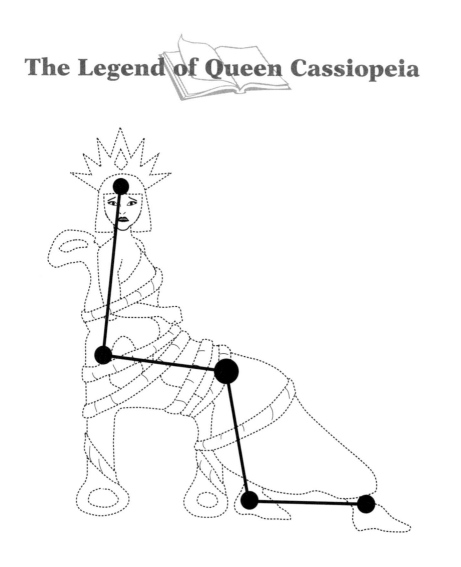

Queen Cassiopeia was the Queen of Ethiopia. She was married to King Cepheus and they had a daughter, Princess Andromeda. Queen Cassiopeia and Princess Andromeda were both very beautiful. This might have been the end of the story, but there was a problem.

Queen Cassiopeia loved to boast. Most of all, she loved to boast about how beautiful she and her daughter were. One day she boasted that she and Andromeda were more beautiful than the Sea-Nymphs, who lived in the ocean. When the Sea-Nymphs heard of this, they were angry! They went to the Sea-God and told him of this terrible insult. He was angry, too! Surely no human could be as beautiful as a Sea-Nymph!

The Sea-God decided he must do something to teach the humans a lesson. So, he created a hideous, snake-like sea monster that would destroy all the humans in Ethiopia. The sea monster paddled along the shore. It stretched its long neck over the land of Ethiopia and snatched and ate people as it swam.

Finally, King Cepheus could take no more. He had to do something to protect the people of his kingdom from the horrible sea monster. He declared war on the monster and ordered his soldiers to shoot the beast with arrows. But the arrows just bounced off the monster's tough scales. Finally, the Sea-God made an announcement to King Cepheus. He declared, "If you want the monster to leave, you must chain your daughter, Princess Andromeda, to the rocks by the sea!"

So, having no other choice, the King did as he was told. He had Andromeda chained to a rock on the shoreline. He stood by sadly to watch as the monster swam along the shore.

Just then, the hero, Perseus, appeared. He flew through the air with his winged sandals. When he saw the beautiful princess chained to the rock, he swooped down to ask what the trouble was. Quickly, Princess Andromeda told him the story. Perseus asked the King and Queen if he could marry the Princess if he killed the sea monster.

They said, " Yes!" So, Perseus soared up into the air with his magic sickle, circled over the monster, swooped down, and cut off the monster's head. He and Princess Andromeda were married the next day. There was a great celebration throughout the land.

When all of these characters died, they were placed comfortably among the stars to tell their story over and over. But to punish Queen Cassiopeia for boasting, she was tied in a chair in a very uncomfortable position. As additional punishment, she had to spend half of the year upside down in the sky! 📖

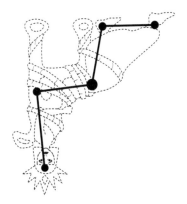

On Your Own

Star Gazing

Your Task
Look at the stars in the night sky for as many nights as possible. Find the Big Dipper, the North Star, and Queen Cassiopeia in the night sky. Record your observations in your journal.

Your Supplies

an adult your science journal your Dipper and Queen Finder 1 copy of Star Map 1 (from Lesson 4)	a flashlight (If you cover the lighted end with a red sock, your eyes won't have to readjust from bright light to the dark, night sky.) your star imagination

Directions for Star Gazing

Watch the stars from the same place each night. Find a place away from bright lights. You might want to star watch at two different times during the evening. Find a landmark, such as a tree or a house, that you can use to describe the position of the stars. Use hand measures to describe how high certain stars are in the sky.

As you watch, draw pictures that show the shape and position of the Big Dipper, Cassiopeia, and Polaris (the North Star). Find out if the shapes and positions of the Big Dipper, Cassiopeia, and the North Star stay the same or change from early to late evening.

After you have watched these stars for several nights, take along a star map to help you find other constellations. Try to find your team's special constellation from Lesson 4. Be prepared to share your drawings and notes with the class.

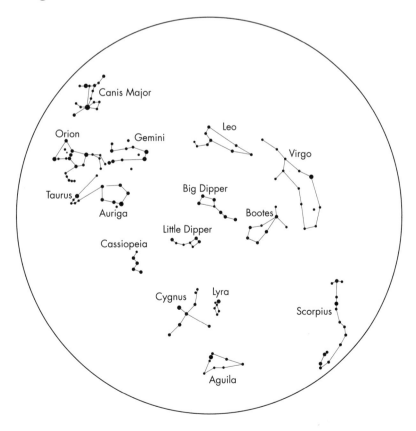

Annie Jump Cannon (1863–1941)

My success, if you would call it that, lies in the fact that I have kept at my work all these years. It is not genius, or anything like that, it is merely patience.

From the time Annie Jump Cannon could climb stairs, she watched the stars. She followed her mother up the stairs—to the attic—through the trapdoor—to the roof of their home. Lying under a big, warm blanket, Annie and her mother watched the sky. They named as many stars as they could. Like her mother, Annie loved gazing at the stars. Before long, Annie had memorized the night sky! She knew almost all the star patterns and the predictable ways the star patterns changed throughout the night and with the seasons.

In school, Annie was a good student. She liked school. But she liked after school best! When she got home and no one was looking, she took a candle from her mother's fancy candelabrum. Then, she snuck up to the attic. By candlelight, Annie read from an old astronomy book and learned all she could about the stars. When Annie's father discovered her secret, he scolded her, "Nothing—not science or the stars—is important enough to risk burning down the house, Annie!" She stopped using the candle to help her read, but she did not stop learning about the stars.

At the time Annie Jump Cannon finished high school, most young women did not go on to college. But, her teachers knew that she was very bright. They thought she should go to college. So did her parents. Annie was eager to go, too.

Ms. Cannon's favorite teacher at college was her science teacher, Miss Sarah Whiting. Professor Whiting was excited about science. Morning and night she took her students onto a rooftop to watch the sky. How Annie Jump Cannon loved rooftops! The closer she was to the sky, the better! While on the rooftop, Professor Whiting taught the students how to use special, new tools to study the stars.

When she finished college, Ms. Cannon returned home. She had planned to do what many educated women did—read and play the piano—but she became bored with that life quickly. Instead, she sailed to Europe and observed a solar eclipse! To remember everything about her trip, she learned photography and took many photographs.

Once back home, Annie Jump Cannon soon became restless. She felt empty. But, why? What was missing? *Rooftops! Telescopes! Photographs! The stars!*

Ms. Cannon became Professor Whiting's assistant. While she was working at the college, she heard of a nearby school that had astronomy classes and an observatory. Before long, Annie Jump Cannon was hired to join other scientists at the Harvard Observatory. She used her sharp eyesight, curiosity, love of the stars, skills in photography, and lots and lots of patience to succeed in her new career.

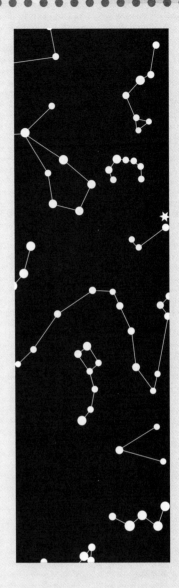

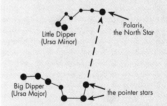

Little Dipper (Ursa Minor)

Polaris, the North Star

Big Dipper (Ursa Major)

the pointer stars

While at the observatory, Ms. Cannon learned to take special photographs of the stars at night. During the day, she looked for surprises—things she did not see with her own eyes—in her photographs of the night sky. Then, she used a telescope to check what she had found. During her lifetime, Annie Jump Cannon made 300,000 photographic plates of the stars—more than anyone else had ever done! She recorded all of her observations, descriptions, and classifications in star catalogs. Through her work, Ms. Cannon became the only woman to hold an honorary degree of Doctor of Science from Oxford University.

Dr. Cannon loved learning about stars. Throughout her adult life, she studied, described, and classified stars so that other people could know more about them, too. Even though many advances have been made in the field of astronomy, scientists today still use the star catalogs made by Annie Jump Cannon and the scientists who worked with her.

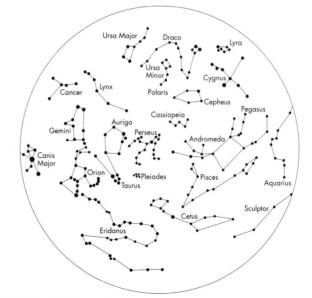

Checking Understanding

Use the notes in your journal to help you answer these questions on your own.

1. Why does the Dipper and Queen Finder show different months and times? (Why do you have to set the Finder in a certain way?)

2. If you watched the stars at two different times during the evening, did the position of the North Star stay the same or did it appear to move?

   (If you could not star gaze at two different times, what do you think would happen to the North Star from one time to the next? Use your Dipper and Queen Finder to help you.)

3. If you watched the stars at two different times during the evening, did the Big Dipper and the Queen look the same or different?

   - How did they look the same?
   - How did they look different?

     (If you could not star gaze at two different times, what do you think would happen to the Big Dipper and the Queen from one time to the next? Use your Dipper and Queen Finder to help you.)

4. Is there a pattern to the way the stars appear to move in the night sky? If so, describe the pattern you see.

Moon Movies

In this module, you have worked like a real astronomer does. First, you observed objects in the sky. Then, you described what those objects looked like, where you found them, and if they changed their position in the sky. You paid careful attention to the changes you saw and recorded your observations in your journal.

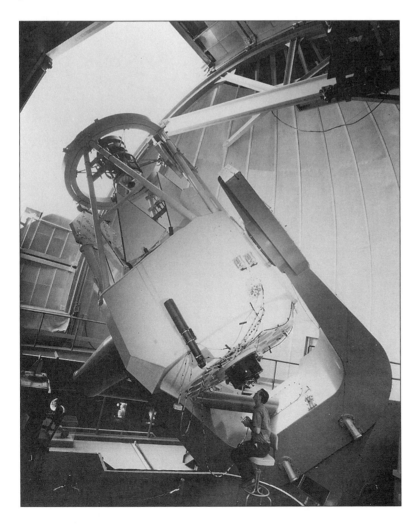

In this lesson, you will use your journal records to find a pattern in the way the Moon looks. By finding a pattern, you can make predictions about how the Moon might look at different times.

Finding Patterns

What is a pattern? Sometimes, a pattern is a design that repeats. You can find design patterns in plants and animals

and in soil and water.

What design patterns did you observe in the sky?

Sometimes, you can find patterns in something that repeats over and over again. The seasons of the year happen in a pattern. What season comes after spring? What season comes after winter? When you know the pattern, you know what will happen next.

What about Moon patterns? Sometimes, you saw the Moon as big, bright, and full.

Sometimes, you saw the Moon as just a sliver.

Is there a pattern to the way the Moon looks at different times? Show what you know by making a "Moon movie." 📖

Making Moon Movies

You recorded a lot of information about how the Moon looks from day to day and night to night. Use your journal and the class charts to help you make a Moon movie.

Team Task

Put pictures of the Moon in order to make a Moon movie flip book. Flip the cards to show how the Moon's appearance changes.

Team Jobs

Manager

Tracker

Messenger

Team Skill

Listen when others talk.

Team Supplies

each teammate's journal	1 set of Moon pictures
3 pairs of scissors	3 pencils
glue	
16 index cards	

Make sure you have 16 moon pictures.

Directions for Making Moon Movies

1. Cut the set of Moon pictures apart.

2. Put the Moon pictures in order.

Remember to listen to your teammates' ideas.

- Use your evidence from the Day and Night Moon Calendars in your journals and on the class charts.

- Talk about how the Moon looked from one day or one night to the next.

- Decide if all your pictures are right side up, not upside down.

3. Make sure everyone agrees with the order of the pictures.

4. When everyone agrees, do these things.

- Talk about where you should place each picture on the index card—top, bottom, left side, right side.

- Glue each Moon picture to an index card.
- Stack the Moon pictures in order.
- Staple the cards together along one end of the stack of cards.

5. Using your thumb and forefinger, flip the index cards and watch your Moon movie!

Let everyone have a turn showing the team's Moon movie.

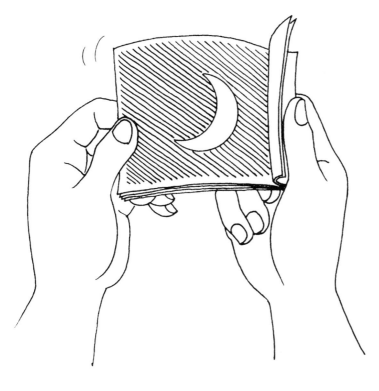

Checking Understanding

Discuss the following questions with your teammates, but write answers in your own journal. Be ready to explain your answers to the class.

1. Watch your Moon movie again. Describe the changes in how the Moon looks.

2. Do the changes show a pattern? If so, describe the pattern.

3. Is this the same pattern you observed and recorded when you watched the Moon? If not, how is it different?

4. Look at these pictures of the Moon. Draw a picture of what you think the Moon will look like next.

5. Do you think the Moon's shape really changes? Why or why not?

 **How Could You Find Out**

- Do you think the pattern in your Moon movie repeats? If so, how often does it repeat? How could you find out?

- After you find out, tell your classmates what you learned.

Patterns in the Sky

In Lesson 6, you made a movie about changes in the way the Moon looks from one day to the next. Describe the pattern you found. Do you think you can find other patterns in the sky?

Using Records to Find Patterns

In this lesson, you will share what you know about patterns in the sky. You will use the evidence you collected in Lessons 2, 3, and 5 to help you.

Your Task
Find your journal records and record pages from Lessons 2, 3, and 5. Use your records to answer questions about the Sun, the Moon, and stars.

Your Supplies

your science journal	1 pencil
record pages from Lessons 2, 3, and 5	
1 Dipper and Queen Finder	

Directions for Using Records to Find Patterns

Use the evidence from your records to answer these questions. Be ready to share your ideas with your classmates.

1. Does the Sun change in any way from morning until evening?

   • If it does, describe how it changes.

   • Does it change in the same way every day?

   • Does the Sun show a pattern in how it changes?

2. Does the Moon change in any way from morning until evening and from evening until morning?

   • What did you discover by watching the Moon during the day and at night?

   • Does the Moon show any patterns other than how it looks from day to day?

3. Do the stars change in any way from evening until morning?

   • Did you find any patterns when you watched the constellations of the Big Dipper, the Little Dipper, and Queen Cassiopeia?

   • Did you observe any patterns when you used the Dipper and Queen Finder?

Making Sky Paths

Have you ever made a path through the mud or snow? How would you describe your path? What did it look like? Could someone have followed your path?

What would a sky path look like for the Sun? the Moon? the Big Dipper? Work with your teammates and find out.

Decide how to show a sky path for the Sun, the Moon, and the Big Dipper. Make a team model. Be ready to add your team's ideas to the class sky paths.

Team Jobs

Manager

Tracker

Messenger

Team Skill

Listen when others talk.

Team Supplies

each teammate's journal	crayons or markers
team record pages	pencils
3 sheets of chart paper	
3 sheets of drawing paper	

Use your record pages from Lesson 3 to help you.

Directions for Making Sky Paths

1. Talk about how the Sun's path across the sky changes from morning until the evening.

2. Draw a picture that shows the Sun's sky path. You may draw your picture on drawing paper or on chart paper. Think about these questions.

- How high in the sky was the Sun at different times of the day?

- Should you show any landmarks in your drawing that help describe where the Sun was in the morning, at noon, and in the afternoon?

Listen to the ideas of your teammates.

3. Repeat Steps 1 and 2 to describe and draw the Moon's sky path.

- Use your journal records, record pages, and the class calendar from Lesson 2 to help you.

- Find your records of the position of the Moon in the sky.

- Describe the change that you observed in the Moon's position.

- Did the Moon change its position from one time to another?
- Did the Moon's sky position change in the same way during the day and at night?
- Draw the Moon's sky path.

4. Repeat Steps 1 and 2 to describe and draw the sky path of the Big Dipper.

  - Use your journal records and the Dipper and Queen Finder from Lesson 5 to help you.
  - Did the Big Dipper change its sky position during the night?
  - If it did, describe how it changed.
  - Then, draw a picture of the sky path of the Big Dipper.

5. Be ready to share your team's drawings with the class.

Sharing
IDEAS

Look at the sky paths drawn by other teams. Are they the same as your team's sky paths?

Do these patterns of movement repeat? How do you know?

Remember to listen when others share their ideas.

Making Models of Patterns in the Sky

Make a classroom model of the sky paths of the Sun, the Moon, and the Big Dipper. How could you show others what you have learned about the sky paths of these objects in the sky?

How Could You Find Out

You have made models of the sky paths of the Sun, the Moon, and the Big Dipper. Here are some questions to think about.

When you cannot see the Sun and the Moon in the sky, where do you think they are?
- Do their sky paths stop?
- Do their sky paths go on?

How would you describe the sky to someone who had never seen it?
- Where is it?
- How far does it go?
- What shape is it?

How would you show the sky on a drawing of Earth?
- Does the Sun really move across the sky?
- Does the Moon really move across the sky?
- Does Earth move in space?

What other questions do you have about the Sun, the Moon, and the stars?

Movement in the Sky...Why?

In this module, you have observed objects in the sky and discovered patterns. Not only have you found a pattern in the way the Moon looks from day to day, you have also found patterns in the changing positions of the Moon, Sun, and stars.

This photograph was taken at night. The photographer pointed the camera toward the North Star and then left the shutter of the camera open for a long time. The white lines are called star trails. They show the paths of the stars through the night. What kind of pattern of movement do the lines show? Is this the same sky path you showed for the stars on the classroom model in Lesson 7?

Have you ever stopped to wonder about objects in the sky?

They Dance in the Sky

A Navajo Indian legend tells why some people long ago thought the constellations moved in the night sky. Read the legend. Try to figure out which stars the legend describes. How did the Navajos explain the movement of the stars?

In the days before the stars were made, the Navajo gods met in their hogan. They had to decide how to make the world and what to put in it. Each god had a special talent and a gift to give to the world. Black God was one of the gods at the meeting. He wore a small group of stars around his ankle. The other gods thought that his stars were so beautiful, they asked him to fill the dark night sky with stars to make it beautiful, too.

Black God agreed. He took out a fawnskin pouch, opened it, and held up a single bright crystal. He reached far out into the sky and carefully placed the crystal in the northern sky. "This is North Fire," he said. "It is the star that shall never move. It will guide the nighttime traveler."

Next he picked out seven great pieces of crystal and placed them near North Fire. As he placed the crystals in the sky he said, "These stars shall be called Revolving Male." After this, Black God placed another set of stars near North Fire. He named this set of stars Revolving Female. "Both Revolving Male and Revolving Female shall always circle North Fire together."

Ideas to Think ABOUT

Which stars did Black God place in the sky?

- What is our name for North Fire?
- What is our name for Revolving Male?
- What is our name for Revolving Female?

How does the legend explain the movement of the stars?

What evidence do you think the Navajos used for the pattern of star movement in this legend?

Astronomy Then and Now

Before the invention of special tools or instruments, people had only their eyes to observe the sky. They watched the sky carefully. They watched the Sun and the Moon. They learned the sky paths of these objects. They charted the changing look of the Moon. They charted stars and learned the pattern of movement of the stars. Just like you, they watched carefully, made notes, and learned the sky patterns very well.

The people of long ago didn't have clocks and calendars to keep track of time. Instead, they learned how to use sky patterns to help them keep track of time. They used the Sun and shadows as a day clock. They used the stars as a night clock. They used the Moon's cycle to make calendars. They knew that when the Moon had gone through its cycle twelve times, one year had passed. Almost all of their planting, harvesting, and celebrations were planned around the movement of the Moon, Sun, and stars.

People of long ago knew a lot about the sky, but they didn't know **why** the objects in the sky appeared to move. They had some ideas to explain what they saw in the sky. They even invented stories and legends to try to explain the patterns of movement they saw. Their ideas, just like the ideas you may have, were good ideas. Their ideas came from what they had observed very carefully.

GALILÉE.

But, movement can be a tricky thing. Sometimes, things that **seem to be moving** really aren't. And things that **don't seem to be moving** really are. Before people had special instruments and tools to help them see into space, they could not find out which objects in the sky really were moving and which just seemed to move.

Over time, scientists have learned a lot about objects in the sky and the movement of those objects. They use special instruments to help them observe. Galileo Galilei was the first to look at the sky through a telescope. When he used his telescope in 1609, he saw incredible things— things such as craters on the Moon, the surface of the Sun, and even tiny moons revolving around a planet. These were things that no one else had ever seen before!

Since Galileo's time, scientists have used even more powerful instruments to learn about objects in the sky. They use these special instruments to make close observations of the objects and to gather lots of information about them. They find out if their information is the same as the information that other scientists have found. Then, they use their information, or data, to find patterns. They use the patterns to make predictions. Making predictions helps scientists find explanations for the patterns in the sky.

Because they have special instruments and tools, they can back up their predictions with evidence. They even can send instruments into space to take pictures. Scientists today have the chance to see and understand why the objects in the sky seem to move. They can find out much more about objects in the sky than people of long ago would have thought possible.

Making a Model of Earth's Neighborhood

You will use what scientists know about objects in the sky and make a model of Earth's neighborhood. Making a model is a good way to learn about things that you cannot really observe. You can learn about the **real** objects by studying the model.

Team Task
Make a model of the Sun, the Moon, and Earth by using Information Clues. Be ready to explain how you think the model of the Sun, Moon, and Earth works.

Team Skill

Share and take turns.

Team Jobs

Manager   Tracker   Messenger

Team Supplies

3 safety pins

Earth nametag

Sun nametag

Moon nametag

1 set of Information Clues

flashlight (optional)

Directions for Making a Model of Earth's Neighborhood

1. Decide which teammate will be the Sun, the Moon, and Earth. Pin on the nametags.

2. Read Information Clue 1 as a team. Do what the clue tells you to do.

3. Read Information Clue 2. Do what the clue tells you to do.

Moon's Path

4. Read Information Clue 3. Do what the clue tells you to do.

Moon's Path

Earth's Path

5. Read Information Clues 4 and 5.

6. Talk to your teammates about what you have learned.

- Be ready to show your team's model of the Earth, Moon, and Sun.

- Be ready to explain what you learned about the movement of Earth, the Moon, and the Sun.

Checking Understanding

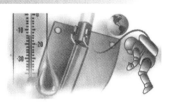

On Your Own

In your journal, draw a model of the Sun, Moon, and Earth.

- Show how they move around one another.
- You can use arrows or lines to show movement.

Below your model, describe how the Sun, Moon, and Earth move.

- Tell which objects in the sky move around another object.
- Tell which object does not move.

With Your Team

Talk about these questions with your teammates. Be ready to share your ideas with the class.

1. Why do you think we have day and night?

   - Which object in the sky is moving to cause day and night?
   - Why do you think so?
   - Model the objects in the sky to show why we have day and night.

     (**Hint:** Darken the room and have the Sun hold a flashlight while you act out the model of Earth's neighborhood.)

2. Does the Sun really move across the sky during the day?

- Why does it look like the Sun moves across the sky?

- What object in the sky is really moving?

3. Do the stars really move in the nighttime sky?

- Why does it look like the stars move in the nighttime sky?

- What object is really moving?

Other Objects in the Sky

So far in this module, you have learned about the positions and movement of the Moon, the Sun, and the stars. What do you know about other objects in the sky?

Do you think there are other objects in the sky besides the ones we can see? I wonder what they look like.

Does this diagram look familiar? This is a diagram of our Solar System. What objects are in the Solar System? What do you know about them?

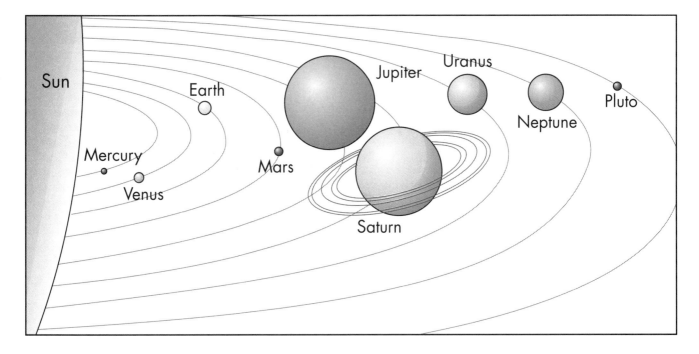

Meet the Planets, Earth's Neighbors in the Sky

Mercury

This rocky, grey planet is the planet closest to the Sun. Because it orbits so close to the sun, Mercury is difficult to observe. But, photographs taken by space probes show that Mercury looks much like our Moon—cratered and without air or water. Mercury has no moons.

Venus

This rocky planet, covered by swirling clouds, is about the same size as Earth. Besides the Sun and Moon, Venus is the brightest object in the sky. It looks like a bright star in the morning or evening. Because of its cloud layers, the surface of Venus is very hot! This planet is hotter than a self-cleaning oven. Venus has no moons.

Earth

Earth is our home. This rocky, blue planet is the only one in our solar system that can support life. Earth has large bodies of water and land masses on its surface. Earth has one Moon.

Mars

Mars is called the "red planet." It has deep, long canyons on its rocky surface and polar ice caps at its north and south poles. There is very little air on Mars. The surface of Mars is very cold! Mars has two moons that orbit the planet.

Jupiter

Jupiter is the largest planet in our Solar System. More than 1,000 Earths could fit inside Jupiter. Jupiter is made of gas and liquid and does not have a solid surface. It appears to have colorful bands across it as well as a Great Red Spot. Sometimes, you can see Jupiter shining in the night sky. Jupiter is the fourth brightest object in the sky after the Sun, the Moon, and Venus. Jupiter has 16 moons.

Saturn

Saturn is also a very large planet, the second largest in the Solar System. Saturn is best known for the beautiful rings that surround it. The planet is made of gas and ice. Its rings are made of billions of tiny pieces of ice. Saturn has 18 moons.

Uranus

This blue-green planet rotates on its side as it orbits the Sun. Because of this, it is always night on one side of the planet. Uranus also has rings, but not as many as Saturn. Uranus has 15 moons.

Neptune

This blue-green planet is made of gas and ice and also has rings like Saturn and Uranus. Scientists discovered Neptune after they noticed that the orbit of Uranus was wobbly. Scientists used mathematics and astronomy to predict, search for, and then discover the planet. Neptune has 8 moons.

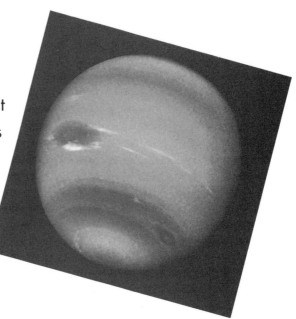

Pluto

Pluto is a tiny planet, not even as big as our Moon. It is made of rock and ice and is the farthest planet from the Sun. Scientists do not agree about whether Pluto is actually a planet or if it is an object in the sky captured from the Kuiper belt, a group of asteroids. Pluto has one moon.

Ideas to Think
ABOUT

In most diagrams of the Solar System, it looks as though the planets are about the same distance from one another. But, the planets are not so evenly spaced from the Sun. Find out how far apart the planets are from one another and from the Sun by making a scale model of the Solar System.

If you make an accurate model, you will need a lot of space from one end of the Solar System to the other!

Distance from the Sun

Planet	Millions of Kilometers	Millions of Miles
Mercury	58	36
Venus	108	67
Earth	150	93
Mars	228	141
Jupiter	778	483
Saturn	1,427	885
Uranus	2,871	1,780
Neptune	4,497	2,788
Pluto	5,914	3,667

You might make a scale model where 1 million kilometers equals 1 centimeter. Then, you can measure each planet's distance from the Sun in centimeters and meters. Does this give you an idea how far apart each planet is from the Sun and from the other planets in space?

Distance from the Sun in the Scale Model

(One million kilometers equals 1 centimeter)

Planet	Millions of Kilometers	Centimeters	Meters
Mercury	58	58	about ½
Venus	108	108	about 1
Earth	150	150	about 1½
Mars	228	228	about 2
Jupiter	778	778	about 8
Saturn	1,427	1,427	about 14
Uranus	2,871	2,871	about 29
Neptune	4,497	4,497	about 45
Pluto	5,914	5,914	about 59

How Could You Find Out

Sometimes, you can see the planets shining in the early morning, early evening, or nighttime sky.

- Which planets can you see without a telescope?
- What is their position in the sky?
- How can you tell them from a star?

You have probably heard about comets, asteroids, black holes, and supernovas.

- Just what are these objects in the sky?
- How could you find out?
- What are other objects in the sky that interest you?

Many objects in the sky were sent into space by people on planet Earth. Some of those objects are satellites, space probes, and Space Shuttles.

- What do you know about these human-made objects in the sky?
- What objects have been sent to study the other planets in the Solar System?
- What information have they sent back to Earth?
- How has this information helped scientists and all of us learn about our Solar System?

What questions do you have about the Solar System, space, and space travel? How could you find out the answers to your questions?

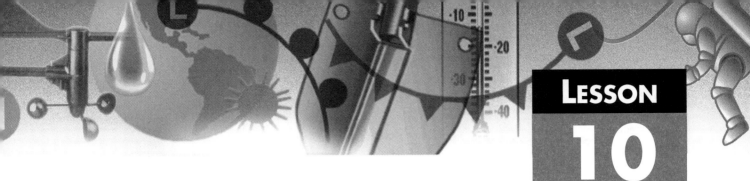

Confusion in Sky Wilderness

Remember the camping trip from Lesson 1? Find the drawing you made about what objects Chloe saw in the sky. Would you draw the sky the same way now?

In this lesson, you will find out how much you have learned about objects in the sky by reading a story. It is not just any story. It is a story filled with mistakes!

What's Wrong in Sky Wilderness?

Have you become sky experts? Do you think your team can find all the mistakes? Read the story and find out!

Team Task
Read the story. Find as many mistakes as you can. Correct the mistakes you find by writing a new sentence or drawing a new picture.

Team Jobs

Manager

Tracker

Messenger

Team Skill

Listen when others talk.

Team Supplies

each teammate's journal   markers or crayons

5 sheets of drawing paper   pencils

Directions for What's Wrong in Sky Wilderness?

1. Read the story out loud.

2. STOP when you come to a numbered sentence.

   - Read the sentence or sentences carefully and look at the picture.

   - Ask yourselves these questions.

Remember to speak softly so only your teammates can hear.

Is the Sun where it belongs?

Does the Sun look the way it should?

Is the Moon where it belongs?

Does the Moon look the way it should?

Are the stars where they belong?

Do the stars look the way they should?

Is the information about the Sun, Moon, and stars correct?

3. In your own journal, write what you think the mistakes are.

- You can use evidence from your journal to help you.

- Share your ideas with your teammates.

4. As a team, write a sentence or sentences that would fix the mistakes.

Remember to listen to your teammates' ideas.

- Make sure everyone agrees with the sentences.

- Copy the sentences into your journal.

5. As a team, draw a new picture that would show the objects in the sky the way they should be.

Listen to everyone's ideas before you begin drawing.

- Use a new sheet of drawing paper for each drawing.

- Sign your names on the drawing.

- Let everyone help with the drawing.

6. Be ready to tell the class how your team fixed the mistakes in the story.

It's Time to Go Home

It was the last day of vacation—the last day of the most wonderful two weeks Chloe could remember. They hiked, played games, roasted marshmallows, and went fishing. They even went for a boat ride on the lake. And, best of all, she had spent lots of time with Dad and Uncle Jordan. Even being with Sam hadn't been too bad.

As Chloe sat up in her sleeping bag, she thought about the camping trip. The most fun had been on the first night when she discovered the doe and fawn under the light of a full moon.

The worst part of the trip had been the fierce mosquitos. Almost every part of Chloe was covered with red, itchy bites. The funniest part had been the night Sam's toy space alien flew into the campfire. Too bad for Sam! The space alien didn't last long in Uncle Jordan's hot fire.

Chloe smiled as she heard Uncle Jordan's voice. "Breakfast is ready, kids," he said softly. "My famous oatmeal with raisins and brown sugar."

"Sounds good," Chloe answered, as she quickly put her clothes on inside her sleeping bag.

"Me, too," Sam replied, still groggy from sleeping.

Chloe stepped out into the morning. She took a deep breath and looked at her watch. It was later than she thought! Almost 8:30! (STOP)

¹ As she looked around, she saw that the Sun was just peeking over the horizon to the west, the North Star was twinkling brightly in the sky, and a quarter moon was setting.

"I think we have time for a hike to the lake after breakfast. Maybe we could fish for a little while. Then, we will have to get everything loaded up and head for home," Dad said as he finished his last bite of oatmeal. "This sure has been a great vacation." His voice trailed off.

"You guys go ahead," Uncle Jordan replied. "I'm going to clean up around here and start packing the truck."

The late morning was beautiful. STOP

² The crescent-shaped Sun appeared to move lower and lower in the sky as it got closer and closer to noon. The full moon shone brightly overhead.

"I guess the fish weren't hungry. No fish today," Sam said, a little disappointedly, as they headed back to the campsite.

When they got back to camp, Uncle Jordan had everything packed and ready to go. "I think all we need to do is check out of the campground, and it's back to civilization," Uncle Jordan sighed.

It was 1:00 in the afternoon as the children climbed into the truck. Chloe hated to leave this place. She looked around at the sky, hoping to remember every part of this vacation. (STOP)

³ The Sun was high in the sky. Chloe noticed that her shadow was very, very long. A crescent-shaped moon was just setting near the horizon.

"Let's get going," Dad announced. "We've got a long drive ahead of us."

Somehow, the drive to Yellowstone had seemed quick. Now, driving home, the time passed very slowly. As the late afternoon Sun warmed the truck, Chloe and Sam fell asleep.

It was 8:00 in the evening when Chloe woke up. "Where are we?" she asked.

"About two hours from home," Dad answered. "How about stopping for some dinner?"

"You bet!" Uncle Jordan and Chloe said at the same time.

Chloe climbed slowly out of the truck. She stretched her arms above her head and looked up at the sky. It was just becoming dark. (STOP)

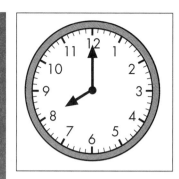

[4] She could not see the Moon, but the Sun was just beginning to rise. A few bright stars twinkled in the sky.

Once back in the truck, the drive home didn't seem to take long.

"Home sweet home," Dad said smiling as they pulled into the driveway. "You guys need to get right to bed. It's 11:00!"

Both Chloe and Sam bounded out of the truck.

"Thanks for a great vacation," Chloe said as she hugged her dad and Uncle Jordan. As she pulled her duffle bag out of the back of the truck, she glanced up at the black, nighttime sky. (STOP)

[5] A crescent moon was setting in the east. She could see the North Star twinkling low in the sky. The Big Dipper, her favorite constellation, was just where she thought it would be — opposite from the North Star on the other side of the sky. She spied Cassiopeia straight overhead, right where it should be! Chloe knew if she came out a few hours later that night, the constellations would be in exactly the same places. They never moved. She knew that even if she couldn't predict where the Sun and Moon would be, she could always count on the stars to stay the same.

Checking Understanding

Choose one of these things to write about in your journal, or tell your teacher if you have another idea about objects in the sky. Use your writing to tell what you have learned about objects in the sky.

1. Write about your favorite object in the sky.

   - Why is it your favorite object in the sky?

   - What do you know about it?

   - What would you like to find out about it?

   - How might you find out?

2. Write about some things you learned about objects in the sky that you did not know before. Write at least three things.

3. Write a letter to an astronomer and tell her or him what you learned about objects in the sky. Tell the astronomer what questions you still have. Maybe the astronomer can help you find answers to your questions!

Acknowledgments

Photo Credits

All photos by Carlye Calvin except as indicated below:

Bob Aguillar by BSCS, p. 112

Corbis-Bettmann, p. 100, p. 105, pp. 124–126

Courtesy of NASA, p. 52, p. 113, p. 115, pp. 134–137

National Center for Atmospheric Research, p. 2 bottom left, p. 3 center, p. 5 top, p. 6 top

Special thanks to the administration, teachers, students, and parents of John Adams Elementary School, Colorado Springs, Colorado, for allowing us to photograph students "doing science." pp. 2–16

Art Credits

Linn Trochim; Brent Sauerhagen, BSCS art files; Laurel Aiello; Dave Blanchette

Design and Prepress

PC&F, Inc., Hudson, New Hampshire

Cover Credits

Comet and telescope images © 1998 PhotoDisc, Inc.
Sun image © Digital Vision